Where in the World Can I . . .

TOUCH A CLOUD?

Where in the World Can I ...

TOUCH A CLOUD?

WORLD
BOOK

www.worldbook.com

World Book, Inc.
180 North LaSalle Street, Suite 900
Chicago, Illinois 60601
USA

For information about other World Book
publications, visit our website at
www.worldbook.com or call
1-800-WORLDBK (967-5325).

For information about sales to schools and
libraries, call 1-800-975-3250 (United States),
or 1-800-837-5365 (Canada).

Library of Congress Cataloging-in-Publication
Data for this volume has been applied for.

Where in the World Can I...
ISBN: 978-0-7166-2178-2 (set, hc.)

Touch a Cloud?
ISBN: 978-0-7166-2188-1 (hc.)

Also available as:
ISBN: 978-0-7166-2198-0 (e-book)

Printed in China by Shenzhen Wing King Tong
Paper Products Co., Ltd., Shenzhen, Guangdong
1st printing July 2018

STAFF

Writer: Shawn Brennan

Executive Committee
President
 Jim O'Rourke

Vice President and
Editor in Chief
 Paul A. Kobasa

Vice President, Finance
 Donald D. Keller

Vice President, Marketing
 Jean Lin

Vice President,
International Sales
 Maksim Rutenberg

Vice President, Technology
 Jason Dole

Director, Human Resources
 Bev Ecker

Editorial
Director, New Print
 Tom Evans

Managing Editor, New Print
 Jeff De La Rosa

Senior Editor, New Print
 Shawn Brennan

Editor, New Print
 Grace Guibert

Librarian
 S. Thomas Richardson

Manager, Contracts &
Compliance (Rights &
Permissions)
 Loranne K. Shields

Manager, Indexing Services
 David Pofelski

Digital
Director, Digital Product
Development
 Erika Meller

Manager, Digital Products
 Jonathan Wills

Graphics and Design
Senior Art Director
 Tom Evans

Coordinator, Design
Development and
Production
 Brenda Tropinski

Media Researcher
 Rosalia Bledsoe

Manufacturing/
Production
Manufacturing Manager
 Anne Fritzinger

Proofreader
 Nathalie Strassheim

TABLE OF CONTENTS

WHAT IS A
CLOUD?

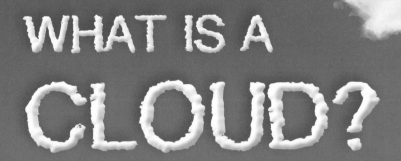

A cloud is a large group of tiny drops of water or pieces of ice that floats in the air. Some clouds look like fluffy white cotton balls. Others look like giant feathers. Still others are gray or black sheets that darken the sky. Most clouds are always changing shape.

Clouds play an important part in Earth's weather. They bring water as rain and snow. This water is needed by all forms of life.

Clouds can also bring dangerous weather, such as hail or tornadoes *(tawr NAY dohz)*. *Hail* is rain that falls as lumps of ice.

7

There are many different kinds of clouds. One type of cloud looks like layers or sheets. These clouds are lower in the sky.

Some clouds are high in the sky and wispy. They look like curls or locks of hair or wool. These clouds are made up of ice crystals.

Other clouds look like fluffy cotton. These clouds grow straight up and down. They are usually seen in fair weather.

10

These fluffy clouds can grow into big, scary clouds that make heavy rain and lightning. These big clouds contain ice crystals. The cloud spreads out into a shape that is wide at the top and narrower at the bottom. This kind of cloud is sometimes called a *thunderhead* because it often causes thunder. Thunder is the rumbling noise we hear after there is a flash of lightning.

Clouds form because the heat of the sun warms lakes, oceans, and rivers. As these waters warm, some of the water changes from liquid water to a gas called *water vapor*.

The water vapor rises into the air. It cools as it rises.

As the water vapor cools, some of it begins to change back into tiny drops of water. If the air is cold enough, the tiny drops of water turn into tiny pieces of ice.

Those drops of water or pieces of ice come together to form clouds.

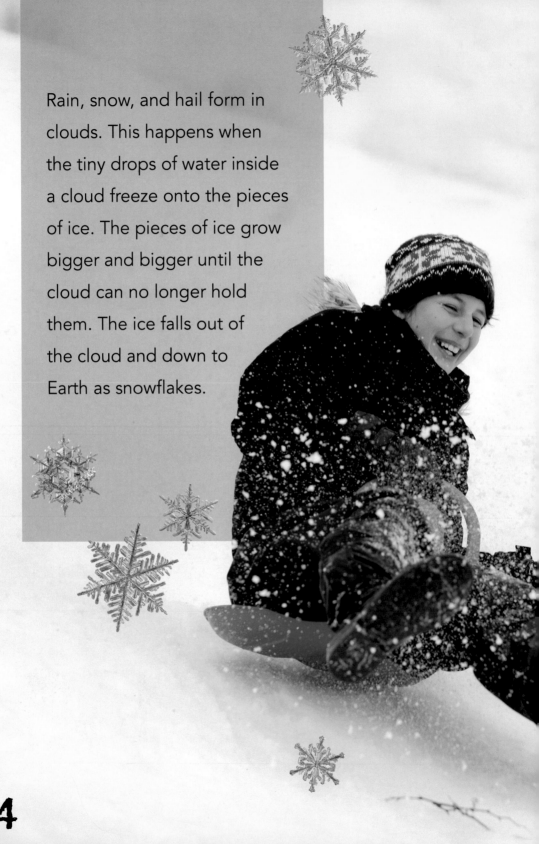

Rain, snow, and hail form in clouds. This happens when the tiny drops of water inside a cloud freeze onto the pieces of ice. The pieces of ice grow bigger and bigger until the cloud can no longer hold them. The ice falls out of the cloud and down to Earth as snowflakes.

But if the ice goes through a layer of air warm enough to melt the snowflake, it falls to Earth as a raindrop. Sometimes the water forms larger pieces of ice called hail. The ice pieces do not melt before they hit the ground. Most often hail is the size of small pebbles. Sometimes, the pieces of ice can grow larger.

The air can rise in several ways. When the sun heats the ground, the air next to the ground is warmed. Because warmer air is lighter than cooler air, the warm air rises, forming a cloud.

16

Clouds also form by *lifting*. When warm, moist air moves up the side of a hill or over a mountain range, it is lifted, and it cools by spreading out. This cooling causes the water vapor to turn into liquid, forming clouds that hang over the mountains.

The lifting of air along weather fronts also creates clouds. A *front* is the boundary between two huge masses of air that have different temperatures.

In fronts where cold air and warm air meet, the warm air rises above the cold air as the cold air slides underneath. As the rising air cools, its water vapor turns into liquid and clouds are formed.

People who *forecast* the weather—tell us what the weather is going to be—study clouds carefully. Certain kinds of clouds often come before a storm. For example, some kinds of clouds come when a warm front moves through an area.

Warm fronts move clouds in a certain order over many days. As these clouds move through an area, they usually bring rain.

Clouds help heat and cool Earth. Cloudy days are usually cooler than clear days. This is because clouds send back sunlight into space. The sunlight does not get a chance to heat Earth. At night, Earth gives off heat toward space. This causes the ground to cool off. Clouds stop much of this heat and send it back toward the ground. So cloudy nights are usually warmer than clear nights. The heat is trapped between the cloud and the ground.

So clouds may look like cotton, feathers, sheets, wool, or hair. But what do they *feel* like? Would you like to touch a cloud? You may have already! Have you ever walked through fog? Fog is like a cloud that touches the ground. There often is fog along seacoasts and lakeshores.

LET'S VISIT SOME OF THE WORLD'S FOGGIEST PLACES!

21

GRAND BANKS— THE FOGGIEST PLACE ON EARTH?

The Grand Banks are a group of underwater plateaus that lie in the Atlantic Ocean off the coast of the Canadian island of Newfoundland (*NOO fuhnd land*). A *plateau* is a raised, flat area. Newfoundland is part of the Canadian province called Newfoundland and Labrador. The province includes the coast of Labrador, a part of the Canadian mainland.

22

The Grand Banks area covers about 139,000 square miles (360,000 square kilometers). The ocean above the Grand Banks is shallow. It is less than 330 feet (100 meters) deep. This area has been called the foggiest place on Earth!

Why is this place so foggy? It is the meeting place of the cold Labrador ocean waters and the much warmer Gulf Stream ocean waters coming up from the south. Warm, moist air moves over the cold water. The water vapor in the warm air above the Gulf Stream suddenly cools and turns into liquid, forming fog.

The mixing of these waters and the shape of the ocean bottom lift *nutrients* to the surface. Nutrients are what living things need to eat to grow. These conditions helped to create one of the richest fishing grounds in the world. Fish that live in the area include cod, flounder, haddock, halibut, herring, and redfish.

Fish began to be caught faster than they could replace themselves. In the late 1900's, the Canadian government placed limits on fish catches in the Grand Banks. Most of the Grand Banks now lies within an area that the government protects against overfishing. This zone stretches 200 *nautical* (sea) miles (370 kilometers) from Canada's coastline.

Boats must have a license from Canada to fish in this zone. Canada also controls the total amount of each kind of fish that fishing boats may take from the Grand Banks.

The waters of the Grand Banks are also rich in *plankton,* small living things that fish like to eat. Sea mammals, including whales and seals, also live in these waters. *Mammals* are warm-blooded animals that feed their young on the mother's milk.

In 1997, oil production began in the deeper water of the Hibernia *(hy BUR nee uh)* oil field on the eastern side of the Grand Banks. Since then, oil companies have developed other oil fields in the same area.

They manage the offshore wells carefully to prevent further endangering fish in this foggy place.

OTHER FOGGY PLACES

SAN FRANCISCO

San Francisco, California, is
a leading center of the
arts, banking, and business
in the United States.

The city is famous for its cable cars, its hills, its
beautiful Golden Gate Bridge—and its fog!

28

Fog often covers the western part of the city.
It forms when warm air flows over the cold
Pacific Ocean water.

However, many people consider the
climate of San Francisco to be ideal. The
temperature rarely rises to 80 °F (27 °C) or
drops to 30 °F (–1 °C).

Water nearly surrounds San Francisco. The Pacific Ocean lies to the west. San Francisco Bay lies to the east. This is why San Francisco is sometimes called the *City by the Bay*. San Francisco is also known as the *City by the Golden Gate*. This is because a *strait* (narrow water channel) called the Golden Gate connects the Pacific Ocean and the San Francisco Bay.

Early European *navigators* (people who choose the direction to sail a ship) probably could not find the Golden Gate strait because of the fogs. These fogs often blanket the Pacific coast for weeks! Spaniards finally reached what now is San Francisco in 1769—by traveling overland!

ATACAMA DESERT

The Atacama
(*at uh KAM uh*) Desert is
in northern Chile and the
southern tip of Peru in
South America. It is one of the
driest places on Earth, but there
is plenty of fog nearby! The desert
begins near Tacna, Chile. It extends
southward about 600 miles (970 kilometers). The
Atacama Desert is bordered on the west by the Pacific
Ocean and on the east by the Andes Mountains.

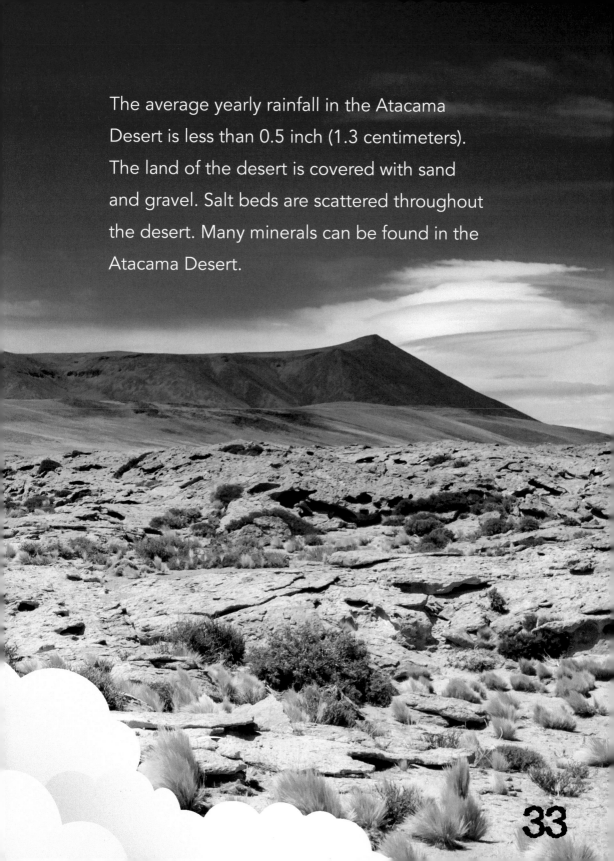

The average yearly rainfall in the Atacama Desert is less than 0.5 inch (1.3 centimeters). The land of the desert is covered with sand and gravel. Salt beds are scattered throughout the desert. Many minerals can be found in the Atacama Desert.

A thick mist called the *camanchaca*
(KAM uhn CHAH kuh) rolls onto the Peruvian
and Chilean coasts from the Pacific. Plants
use the fog for nourishment. People have
also figured out ways to collect water from
the fog as it rolls over the mountains.

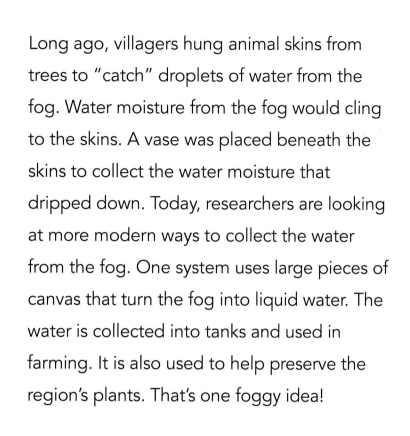

Long ago, villagers hung animal skins from trees to "catch" droplets of water from the fog. Water moisture from the fog would cling to the skins. A vase was placed beneath the skins to collect the water moisture that dripped down. Today, researchers are looking at more modern ways to collect the water from the fog. One system uses large pieces of canvas that turn the fog into liquid water. The water is collected into tanks and used in farming. It is also used to help preserve the region's plants. That's one foggy idea!

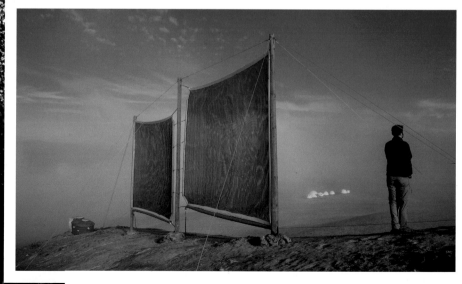

NAMIB DESERT

Another "foggy" desert near an ocean is the Namib (*NAH mihb*) Desert. It lies along southern Africa's west coast, mostly in the country of Namibia (*nuh MIHB ee uh*). The desert covers more than 31,200 square miles (80,900 square kilometers). It extends from the Orange River in the south to the country of Angola (*an GOH luh*) in the north. The Atlantic Ocean is the western limit. Steep slopes make up the eastern edge.

Offshore fog collides with warm air to create clouds that surround the Namib Desert. The coast has more than 180 days of thick fog a year. But it receives less than ¾ inch (2 centimeters) of rain a year.

The Skeleton Coast forms part of the northern region of the desert. It received its name because of the many shipwrecks that occurred there. Fog caused many of these shipwrecks! Ships crashed into the beaches because sailors could not see the land.

SMOKE + FOG = SMOG

Smog is one type of fog we don't want around us! Smog is a kind of *air pollution (puh LOO shuhn)* (dirtying of the air). Smog is a hazy mixture of gases and tiny bits of matter. *Matter* is the substance, or material, from which all things are made. Smog can cause breathing problems in humans and animals. It can kill plants and break down building materials. Many of the world's cities are polluted by smog.

The word *smog* is a combination of *smoke* and *fog.* It was first used in 1905 to describe the kind of air pollution that at times hung over London and other cities in the United Kingdom. The smog resulted from the burning of coal. This kind of smog contains a type of gas that can make breathing difficult.

A terrible smog in 1952 killed about 4,000 Londoners. Work by the central government and local authorities helped clean up London's badly polluted air. *Parliament* (Britain's lawmaking body) passed Clean Air acts in 1956, 1968, and 1993. These acts limited the use in London of fuels that make smoke. This resulted in cleaner air.

39

Air pollution can also mix with water vapor in the air. This mixing can result in *acid rain*. Acid rain is harmful rain that contains levels of acids higher than normal. Acid rain harms lakes and rivers and kills fish and other wildlife. Scientists believe acid rain also damages forests, soil, statues, bridges, and buildings.

1908

present

Another kind of smog
is caused by chemicals
released from cars
and factories. Sunlight
changes these
chemicals into smog.

41

Air pollution can change Earth's atmosphere in harmful ways. Burning fuel creates *greenhouse gases* that hold in heat like the glass walls of a greenhouse. Such gases are a cause of *global warming*, a rise in Earth's average temperature.

Researchers have linked global warming to damage to living things and their ecosystems. An *ecosystem* is a community of living things along with its physical surroundings, or environment.

Global warming is raising the level of the sea. It is also changing the Arctic region by melting the ice there. Global warming may also change weather patterns and affect human health around the world. Scientists believe that these effects will grow worse and spread with further warming.

Most countries have national pollution control agencies. Many countries have also agreed to work together to fight global warming. Many of them are taking steps to cut the amount of greenhouse gases entering the atmosphere. Some countries are using more energy from the sun or the wind to reduce the amount of fossil fuels being burned. Scientists are also working to make machines that use less fuel.

We can do our part to help reduce air pollution and limit global warming, too. For example, walking or riding bikes instead of driving helps reduce air pollution.

So does carpooling or taking public transportation.
Using more efficient cars also helps. People can
also use less heat and electric power in their homes
and buildings by turning off lights and electric

BOOKS AND WEBSITES

BOOKS

Clouds by Anne Rockwell (Collins, 2008)
Includes basic facts and details about the 10 types of clouds and the kind of weather connected with each type. You can also learn how to make a cloud of your own!

The Man Who Named the Clouds by Julie Hannah and Joan Holub (Albert Whitman, 2006)
This colorful book balances biographical information about British chemist Luke Howard, who proposed a classification system for clouds in 1802, with basic weather science. Includes a bibliography.

A Party for Clouds: Thunderstorms by Belinda Jensen (Lerner/Millbrook, 2016)
Fictional narrative combines with playful cartoon illustrations to frame facts about storms and weather events. Includes activities.

WEBSITES

Explore the Atmosphere
http://cimss.ssec.wisc.edu/wxfest/

On this website, kids can explore the atmosphere with fun weather and climate activities.

SPARK: Games for Weather, Climate and Atmospheric Science Education
https://scied.ucar.edu/games

This site from the University Corporation for Atmospheric Research includes a collection of games, interactive activities, and simulations related to weather.

Thirstin's Water Cycle
http://www.epa.gov/safewater/kids/flash/flash_watercycle.html

In this animated activity created by the EPA, students learn as they control the water cycle.

Web Weather for Kids
http://eo.ucar.edu/webweather/

Includes activities and information on thunderstorms, tornadoes, hurricanes, blizzards, and clouds. Students can also create simulations of different types of weather.

INDEX

47

ACKNOWLEDGMENTS

Cover: © Zorazhuang/iStockphoto; © Olesia Bilkei, Shutterstock; © Effective Stock Photos/Shutterstock

2-5 © Shutterstock

6-7 © MediaProduction/iStockphoto; © Shutterstock

8-13 © Shutterstock

14-15 © Akrp/iStockphoto; © Shutterstock

16-23 © Shutterstock

24-25 © Orchidpoet/iStockphoto; © Shutterstock

26-27 © iStockphoto; © Design Pics Inc/Alamy Images; © Shutterstock

28-29 © Francesco Carucci, Shutterstock

30-31 © Atosan/Dreamstime; © Balla Family Group/ Shutterstock

32-33 © Shutterstock

34-35 © Anky/Shutterstock; © Martin Bernetti, AFP/Getty Images

36-37 © Shutterstock

38-39 © iStockphoto; © Vjom/Shutterstock; © Central Press/Getty Images

40-41 © Shutterstock; E. M. Winkler, Stone: Properties, Durability in Man's Environment

42-45 © Shutterstock